PATTERN PIECES

Can you help each child find the pieces that match the ones in his or her pattern? Each piece goes to only one pattern.

Answer on page 48

Illustration: John Nez

3

OVER IN THE MEADOW

Illustration: David Helton

Match each butterfly with its cocoon.

Answer on page 48

DIAMOND IN THE ROUGH

The numbers 1 to 9 go in the circles of this diamond. Use the clues to help you figure out where each number belongs. When you are done, enter each circle only once to find a path that will lead from 1 to 9 in order.

1. The lowest and highest numbers are next to each other in the same row across.
2. The numbers in the top circle and the bottom circle are both odd.
3. There are no odd numbers in the second or fourth rows.
4. The number that is halfway between 1 and 9 is in the right-hand circle of the center row.
5. The two numbers in the second row across equal the number in the second circle of the fourth row.
6. When you subtract the 1 from the number to its left, the answer goes in the left-hand circle in the next row down.
7. The bottom left side of the diamond contains the three highest numbers in descending order from the center row to the bottom.
8. If you started counting at the top and then counted left to right in each row, 2 is the only number that appears in numerical order.

Illustration: Paul Richer

Hint on page 46

Answer on page 48

TREE STUMPER

This forest ranger wants to know which of these stumps belongs to the oldest tree. She knows that each ring equals one year. Can you count the rings on each stump to find which came from the oldest tree?

Illustration: R. Michael Palan

MARBLE MYSTERY

Can you tell the one thing that each group has in common?

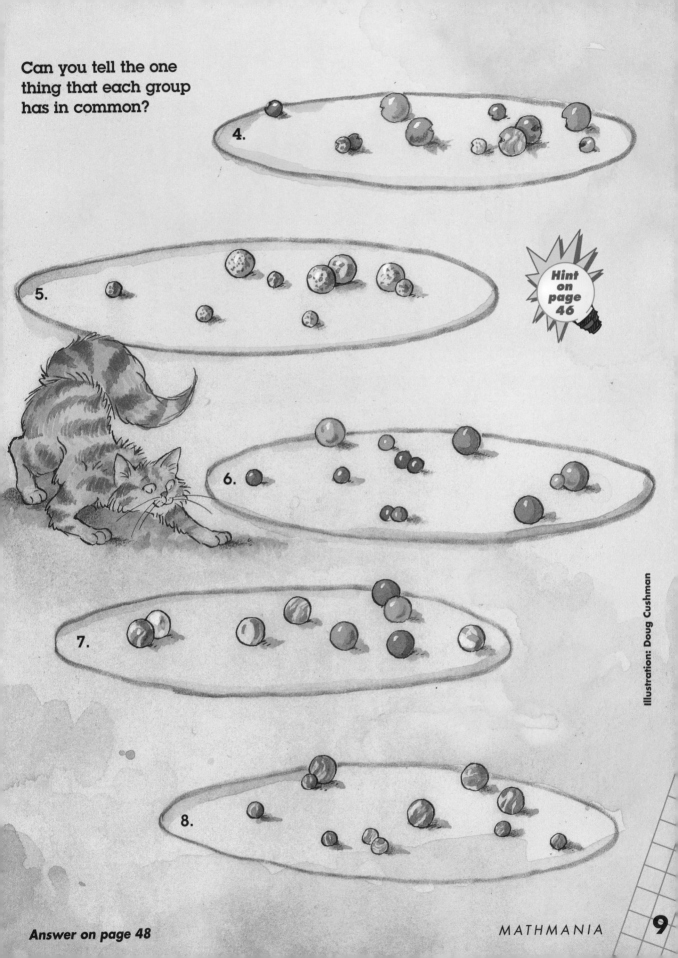

4.

5.

Hint on page 46

6.

7.

8.

Illustration: Doug Cushman

Answer on page 48

CIRCLE 17

Hint on page 46

Using only three straight lines, can you divide the circle into 7 sections so that the numbers in each section total 17? A section can hold either one, two, three, or four numbers.

Illustration: Marc Nadel

Answer on page 48

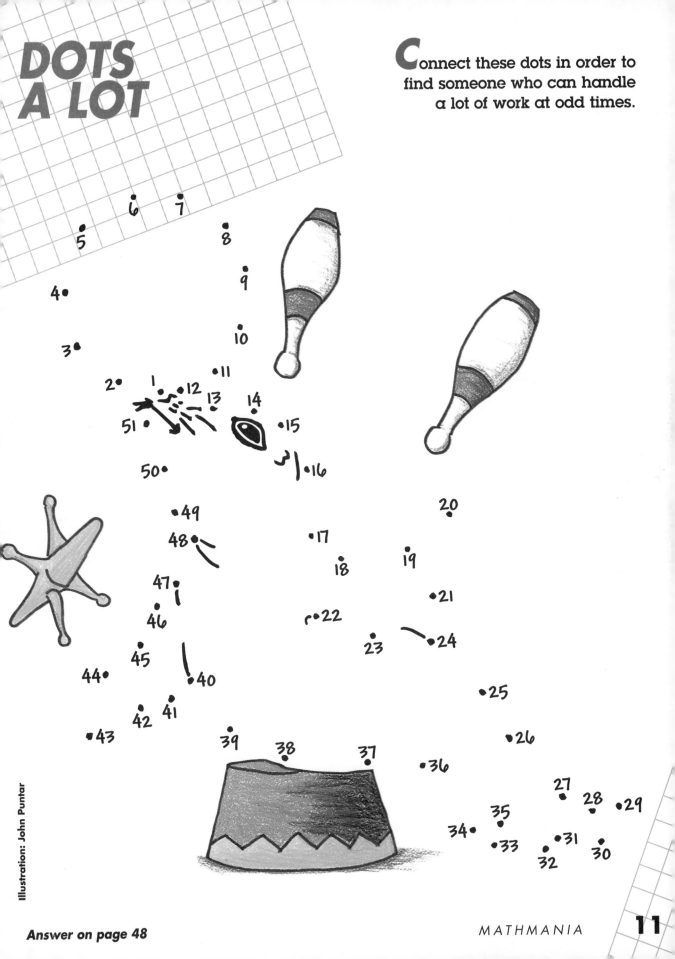

DOTS A LOT

Connect these dots in order to find someone who can handle a lot of work at odd times.

Illustration: John Puntar

DOGGIE DELIVERY

To find the answer to this delivery person's riddle, look at the letters. Follow the instructions, solving the math problems and gathering letters along the way.

1. The first letter is in the upper left corner.

2. To find the second letter, move 6 – 1 letters to the right.

3. The next letter is 2 + 3 + 3 letters down.

4. Gather your next letter by moving 28 – 24 letters to the right.

5. You'll find the next letter 20 ÷ 5 letters up.

6. The next letter is 36 ÷ 4 letters to the left.

7. Move 30 – 25 letters down to the next letter.

8. The next letter is 33 ÷ 11 letters to the right.

9. This letter can be found 49 ÷ 7 letters up.

10. Pick up the next letter by moving 24 ÷ 8 letters to the right.

11. The last letter can be found 17 – 12 letters down.

Place the letters in the blanks in the order you fetch them. For each new clue, begin counting from your previous letter.

```
M A N T X U R S N L
Y R O O V B K X D A
S E L L G C L U I P
Z Y K H E E O N C R
A Y E W N H M C S S
H F O I L B A C T R
R G A E S R B D X N
E M B Y T T A W G I
Y F R E S T N P E T
R N U E V K L X B M
```

Illustration: Jerry Zimmerman

What do dogs like on their pizza?

___ ___ ___ ___ ___ ___ - ___ ___ ___ ___ ___

FUNCTION MACHINES

Each machine has a specific function. When a number goes into the column on the left, the machine performs its function and a new number is revealed on the right. Figure out the function for each machine, and then fill in the missing numbers.

Hint on page 46

Illustration: Rick Geary

Answer on page 49

FAMOUS NAME

Hint on page 46

If you connect the dots in the order listed, you will find the name of the person described in this autobiography.

I was born in Edinburgh, Scotland, on November 13, 1850. When I was 17, I entered Edinburgh University. It was the same year my first piece of writing was published. Over my lifetime, I wrote many stories and numerous poems that are still enjoyed today.

Illustration: Kit Wray

```
    A  B  C  D  E  F  G  H  I  J  K  L  M  N  O  P  Q  R  S  T  U  V
1   .  .  .  .  .  .  .  .  .  .  .  .  .  .  .  .  .  .  .  .  .  .
2   .  .  .  .  .  .  .  .  .  .  .  .  .  .  .  .  .  .  .  .  .  .
3   .  .  .  .  .  .  .  .  .  .  .  .  .  .  .  .  .  .  .  .  .  .
4   .  .  .  .  .  .  .  .  .  .  .  .  .  .  .  .  .  .  .  .  .  .
5   .  .  .  .  .  .  .  .  .  .  .  .  .  .  .  .  .  .  .  .  .  .
6   .  .  .  .  .  .  .  .  .  .  .  .  .  .  .  .  .  .  .  .  .  .
```

A1-A3 B1-B2 C1-C3 D1-D3 E1-E3 F1-F3 G1-G3 I1-I3 J1-J2 L1-L3 N1-N3 P1-P3
Q1-Q3 R1-R3 S1-S3 T1-T3 U1-U2 V2-V3 A4-A5 B5-B6 D4-D6 F4-F6 K4-K6 M4-M6
O4-O6 P4-P5 Q5-Q6 R4-R6 S4-S6 T4-T6 V4-V6 A1-B1 A2-B2 A4-B4 A5-B5 A6-B6
C1-D1 C3-D3 C4-E4 E1-F1 E2-F2 E3-F3 F4-G4 F5-G5 F6-G6 G1-H1 G2-H2 G3-H3
I1-J1 I2-J2 K4-L4 K5-L5 K6-L6 K1-M1 N3-O3 P1-Q1 P3-Q3 P4-Q4 P5-Q5 P6-Q6
U1-V1 U2-V2 U3-V3 A2-B3 I2-J3 H4-I6 I6-J4 M4-O6 T4-V6 R3-S3 R4-S4 R6-S6

WATCH THE DIFFERENCE

Each watch or clock below shows a time that's after noon but before midnight. First figure out the difference in time between each pair of timepieces. Write that time difference in the space

O

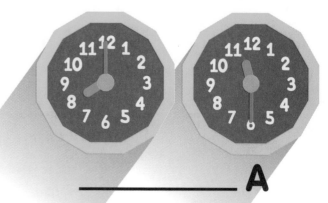

A

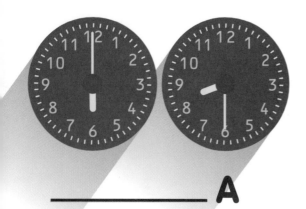

A

D

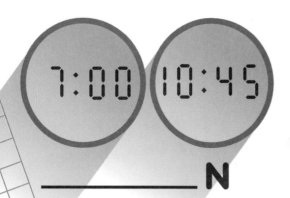

N

K

Illustration: Paul Richer

underneath the pair. You'll see a
letter with each pair. Write those
letters in order, going from the pair
with the smallest time difference to
the pair with the greatest difference,
into the blanks below the riddle.

_____ **H**

_____ **N**

_____ **S**

_____ **O**

_____ **M**

_____ **L**

_____ **O**

Hint on page 46

What did the digital clock say to its mother?

__ __ __ __ , __ __ ! __ __ __ __ __ __ __ __ !

Answer on page 49

STACKING STANLEY

Stanley has to deliver two barrels of soda to each customer. But he forgot to write down the two flavors each customer wanted.

Luscious Lime
31 liters

SACK-O

Strawberry Fizz
27 liters

Cheery Cherry
30 liters

Go-go Grape
22 liters

Lefty Lemon
40 liters

Orange Slurp
35 liters

Answer on page 49

Order 1: Pop's Chocklit Shoppe   50 liters _____ _____
Order 2: Arnold's   75 liters _____ _____
Order 3: Mel's Diner   52 liters _____ _____
Order 4: Louie's Sweet Shop   60 liters _____ _____

Can you look at the amounts ordered and figure out where each barrel should go?

Hint on page 46

DELIVERY

ACME
DELIVERY

DELIVE

ACM
DELIVE

Berry Bubble
23 liters

Rah-rah Root Beer
29 liters

Sac

Illustration: R. Michael Palan

19

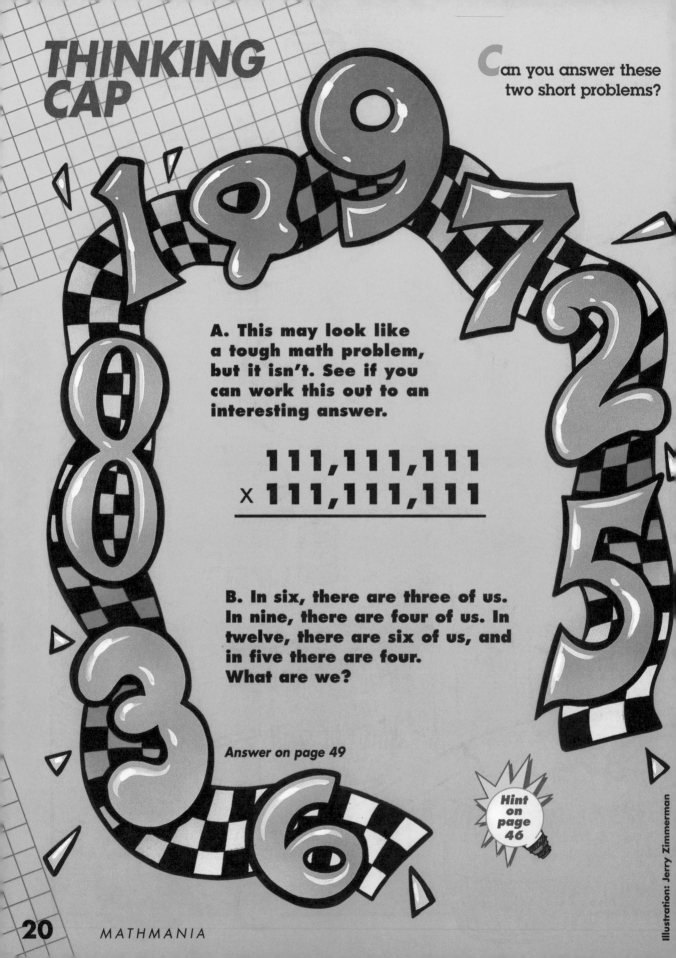

THINKING CAP

**A. This may look like
a tough math problem,
but it isn't. See if you
can work this out to an
interesting answer.**

$$111,111,111 \times 111,111,111$$

**B. In six, there are three of us.
In nine, there are four of us. In
twelve, there are six of us, and
in five there are four.
What are we?**

Answer on page 49

**Hint
on
page
46**

Illustration: Jerry Zimmerman

ODD ORDER

These books all fell off the shelf. Look at the page numbers to put the books back in order. Volume 1 starts at page 1, and Volume 10 ends at page 510. Once you have the order, read the letter next to the number on each right-hand page. You'll find a ten-letter word that starts with G-A-S.

37 A

36

112

113 T

361 B

360

509 E

405 I

08

477 L

333 O

211 O

94

299 M

95 U

Illustration: Jim Downer

DIGIT DOES IT

Answer on page 49

But he found a coded clue.
Can you decipher the message
and help the Inspector
collect the evidence?

$\overline{1}\ \overline{3}\ \overline{14}\ \overline{16}$ $\overline{15}\ \overline{6}\ \overline{18}\ \overline{10}\ \overline{3}\ \overline{7}\ \overline{20}\ \overline{8}\ \overline{16}$ $\overline{1}\ \overline{15}\ \overline{9}\ \overline{15}\ \overline{20}$,

$\overline{15}$ $\overline{19}\ \overline{2}\ \overline{3}\ \overline{22}$ $\overline{20}\ \overline{12}\ \overline{3}$ $\overline{7}\ \overline{8}\ \overline{8}\ \overline{10}$, $\overline{18}\ \overline{8}$

$\overline{20}\ \overline{12}\ \overline{3}$ $\overline{13}\ \overline{8}\ \overline{2}\ \overline{17}\ \overline{18}$ $\overline{8}\ \overline{6}$ $\overline{13}\ \overline{8}\ \overline{5}$.

$\overline{15}$ $\overline{4}\ \overline{14}\ \overline{6}\ \overline{14}\ \overline{9}\ \overline{3}\ \overline{1}$ $\overline{20}\ \overline{8}$ $\overline{12}\ \overline{15}\ \overline{1}\ \overline{3}$ $\overline{L}\ \overline{G}$

$\overline{3}\ \overline{9}\ \overline{9}\ \overline{18}$ $\overline{14}\ \overline{19}\ \overline{20}\ \overline{3}\ \overline{16}$ $\overline{15}$ $\overline{12}\ \overline{14}\ \overline{20}\ \overline{7}\ \overline{12}\ \overline{3}\ \overline{1}$

$\overline{20}\ \overline{12}\ \overline{15}\ \overline{18}$ $\overline{10}\ \overline{2}\ \overline{14}\ \overline{6}$, $\overline{13}\ \overline{8}\ \overline{5}\ \overline{2}\ \overline{2}$ $\overline{12}\ \overline{14}\ \overline{11}\ \overline{3}$

$\overline{20}\ \overline{8}$ $\overline{18}\ \overline{7}\ \overline{16}\ \overline{14}\ \overline{4}\ \overline{21}\ \overline{2}\ \overline{3}$ $\overline{20}\ \overline{8}$ $\overline{19}\ \overline{15}\ \overline{6}\ \overline{1}$

$\overline{20}\ \overline{12}\ \overline{3}\ \overline{4}$ $\overline{14}\ \overline{2}\ \overline{2}$.

$\overline{14}\ \overline{2}$ $\overline{21}\ \overline{5}\ \overline{4}\ \overline{3}\ \overline{6}$

Hint on page 46

Illustration: Joe Boddy

CUTUPS

Lumber Jackie has three small red squares that are equal in size. She wants to make only two cuts and rearrange the pieces to make one complete red square. Can you show her where to cut?

Illustration: Rocky Fuller

Hint
on
page
47

Answer on page 49

ALL IN A DAY

Jessica divided up her day as shown. Can you use the chart to answer each question?

Hint on page 47

VOLUNTEER
2 Hours

SCHOOL
6 Hours

SLEEP
10 Hours

PLAY
3 Hours

HOMEWORK
1 Hour

PIANO PRACTICE
1 Hour

MEALS
1 Hour

1. What section takes up the biggest part of Jessica's day?
2. What percentage of the day does Jessica spend in school?
3. What is the total number of hours Jessica spends on school-related things?
4. If Jessica goes to bed at 8 p.m., what time does she wake up?
5. Does Jessica spend more time playing or volunteering?
6. Which three sections, when added together, equal the same amount of time as Jessica's play section?

Illustration: Don Robison

SCRAMBLED PICTURE

Copy these mixed-up rectangles onto the next page to unscramble the picture.

A-3   A-4   A-1   A-2

B-2   B-4   B-1   B-3

C-4   C-1   C-3   C-2

D-4   D-3   D-2   D-1

The letters and numbers tell you
where each rectangle belongs. We've
done the first one, A-3, to start you off.

Answer on page 50

LIBRARY LAUGHS

Dewey has some funny books in his library. To check one out, solve each problem. Then go to the shelves to find the volume with the number that matches each answer. Put the matching letter in the blank beside each answer. Read down the letters you've filled in to find the title and author of the book Dewey just finished reading.

A 1   N 14   J 10   Y 25

F 6   V 22   S 19   U 21   B 2   C 3   D 4   E 5   P 16   G 7   R 18   X 24   T 20

L 12   M 13   W 23   Q 17   H 8   K 11

Z 26   O 15   I 9

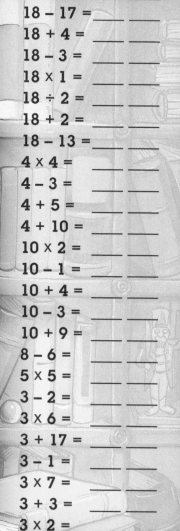

Illustration: Scott Peck

Answer on page 50

Hint on page 47

$18 \div 3 =$ _____

$18 - 17 =$ _____

$18 + 4 =$ _____

$18 - 3 =$ _____

$18 \times 1 =$ _____

$18 \div 2 =$ _____

$18 + 2 =$ _____

$18 - 13 =$ _____

$4 \times 4 =$ _____

$4 - 3 =$ _____

$4 + 5 =$ _____

$4 + 10 =$ _____

$10 \times 2 =$ _____

$10 - 1 =$ _____

$10 + 4 =$ _____

$10 - 3 =$ _____

$10 + 9 =$ _____

$8 - 6 =$ _____

$5 \times 5 =$ _____

$3 - 2 =$ _____

$3 \times 6 =$ _____

$3 + 17 =$ _____

$3 - 1 =$ _____

$3 \times 7 =$ _____

$3 + 3 =$ _____

$3 \times 2 =$ _____

PHONE FUN

Phyllis wanted to spend less than $50 for February's phone calls. Use the phone company's rates to figure out her phone bill. Did she meet her goal?

Illustration: Bill Colrus

PHONE BILL

DATE	STARTING TIME OF CALL	MINUTES TALKED	COST
Monday, 2/1	1:05 p.m.	35	___
Wednesday, 2/3	7:33 p.m.	56	___
Friday, 2/5	11:45 a.m.	5	___
Saturday, 2/6	10:57 a.m.	65	___
Tuesday, 2/9	8:14 p.m.	42	___
Friday, 2/12	6:22 p.m.	90	___
Sunday, 2/14	7:30 a.m.	5	___
Monday, 2/15	6:30 a.m.	10	___
Thursday, 2/18	12:05 p.m.	20	___
Sunday, 2/21	3:27 p.m.	35	___
Tuesday, 2/23	5:15 p.m.	45	___
Friday, 2/26	1:07 p.m.	23	___
		TOTAL	

COMPANY RATES

Monday through Friday —
12:01 a.m. to 5:00 p.m.: $.25 per minute
5:01 p.m. to 12:00 midnight: $.10 per minute

Saturday and Sunday — $.05 per minute

Hint on page 47

IT FIGURES

A

B

C

D

E

F

that figure. The two figures that have the same number of blocks are a match. Can you find all seven pairs?

I

H

J

G

K

L

M

N

Illustration: Doug Cushman

MATHMAGIC

Have a friend choose any five-digit number. How about 53,897?

Now have him choose any other five-digit number.

Let's say 71,532.

Now the challenge is to multiply the two numbers together faster than your friend can.

You don't want the full answer. You only want to know if the answer is going to be odd or even.

Ready? Multiply.

The answer this time is: even!

Hint on page 47

To find out how to win every time, check out page 50.

Illustration: Marc Nadel

SAND ART

Can you draw this figure without crossing over or going back along any lines?

Illustration: Barbara Gray

Answer on page 50

33

MAP MILES

Myles Tugo is hitting the road. Can you look at his map and help

Hint on page 47

Trip 1—Eagle Tower to Sandtown   _____ miles

Trip 2—Wood to Lakeside   _____ miles

Trip 3—Blue City to Cedar Springs   _____ miles

Trip 4—Big Bay to Blufftown   _____ miles

Trip 5—Rapid River to Rockville   _____ miles

Illustration: Scott Peck

him add up the shortest
routes between the towns
he will visit?

Answer on page 50

FUNNY FRACTIONS

To figure out our definition for today's word, find the letters described by the clues. Then write the letters in the blanks, going from left to right in order.

Today's word:

DISGUISE

Last $\frac{3}{4}$ of HAIR
First $\frac{5}{6}$ of PLANET
First $\frac{5}{7}$ of SANDBOX
Last $\frac{2}{3}$ of THIRDS
Middle $\frac{1}{2}$ of OBEY
First $\frac{1}{2}$ of LONGITUDES
Last $\frac{3}{5}$ of NINTH
Middle $\frac{1}{2}$ of FISH

Illustration: R. Michael Palan

Answer on page 50

COLOR BY NUMBERS

Illustration: Rob Sepanak

1 dot—Peach
2 dots—Beige
3 dots—White
4 dots—Dark Blue
5 dots—Light Blue
6 dots—Red
7 dots—Orange

Use the key to color the shapes.

Answer on page 50

ON THE SQUARE

Match each shape with a number from 1 to 10, based on the number of rectangular land parcels in each shape.

B

A

Hint on page 47

C

D

E

F

G

H

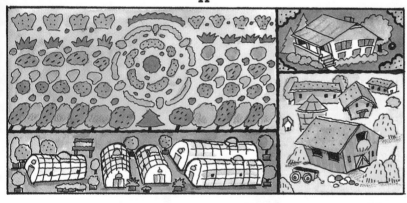

I

SUNFLOWER FARM

J

Answer on page 51

RAINBOW REPORT

Hint on page 47

Alice's dad promised her a pair of new skates if she earned an 80 or above in each school subject. Instead of writing number grades, Alice's teacher placed color blocks by each subject. Use the color code to see if Alice is in line for some new wheels. She'll also get a new calculator if her overall average is 85 or better. Can you tell if she reached her goal?

KEY

Color	Value
Blue	50
Yellow	110
Light Green	28
Orange	57
Purple	19
Red	99
Brown	42
Dark Green	63

REPORT CARD

Math ▢ + ▢ _____

Language Arts ▢ + ▢ + ▢ _____

Science ▢ – ▢ _____

Social Studies ▢ + ▢ _____

Gym ▢ + ▢ _____

Art (▢ – ▢) + ▢ _____

Spanish (▢ + ▢) – ▢ _____

Illustration: Anni Matsick

Answer on page 51

MASS MATH

Julio is doing a project on the mass of the planets. The numbers shown are not actual pounds. Instead, each number represents the amount of matter in an object, based in relation to Earth, which is considered 1. For example, scientists believe Neptune has 17.15 times more mass than Earth. You can help Julio by putting the planets in order from the smallest to the greatest in mass. Then read the letters on each planet in order to find out what interplanetary architects use to build houses on other planets.

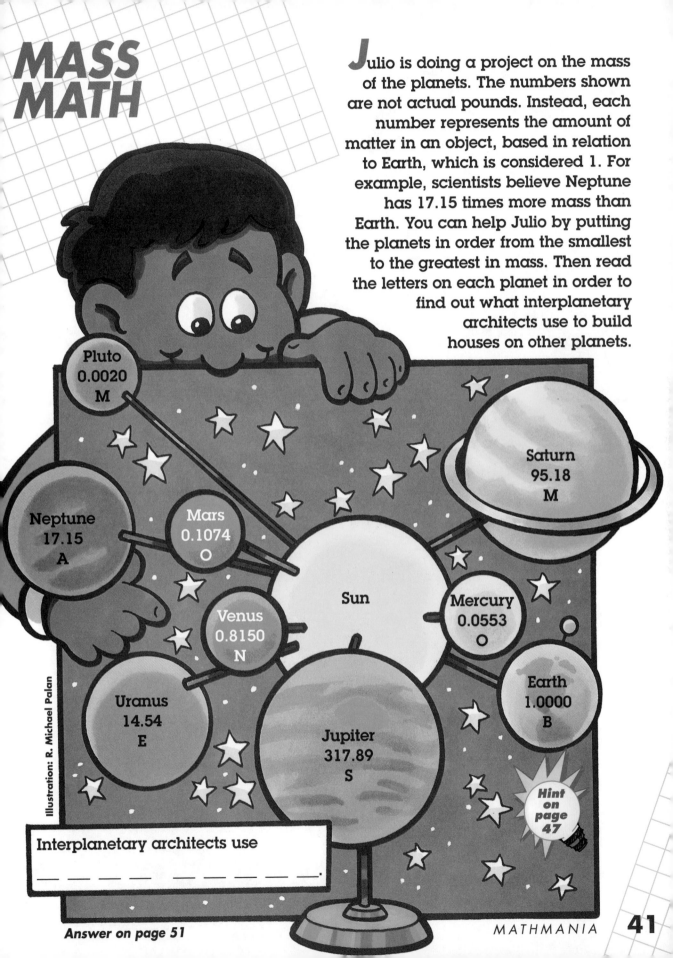

Pluto
0.0020
M

Saturn
95.18
M

Neptune
17.15
A

Mars
0.1074
O

Venus
0.8150
N

Sun

Mercury
0.0553
O

Uranus
14.54
E

Jupiter
317.89
S

Earth
1.0000
B

Hint on page 47

Interplanetary architects use

_ _ _ _ _ _ _ _ _ _ .

Illustration: R. Michael Palan

Answer on page 51

SHAPE MAZE

START 1000

in each new shape.
Follow the path and use
the key to guide you.

KEY

10 greater

10 less

100 greater

100 less

1000 greater

1000 less

Illustration: Don Robison

Hint
on
page
47

Answer on page 51

MATHMANIA

LIQUID LINEUP

Circle the larger amount in each pair of measurements. Use the conversion chart to help you decide. When you're finished, write the circled letters in the blanks to find the quickest way to make oil boil.

CONVERSION CHART

1 tablespoon = 3 teaspoons
1 fluid ounce = 2 tablespoons
1 cup = 8 fluid ounces
1 pint = 2 cups
1 quart = 2 pints
1 gallon = 4 quarts

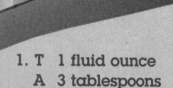

5. H 9 teaspoons
   M 2 tablespoons

1. T 1 fluid ounce
   A 3 tablespoons

2. D 5 cups
   H 1 quart

3. E 2 gallons
   D 9 quarts

4. R 8 cups
   T 3 quarts

6. E 2 gallons
   O 15 pints

7. D 1 cup
   L 20 fluid ounces

8. E 15 pints
   Y 26 cups

9. T 3 pints
   N 1 quart

10. A 5 cups
    T 48 fluid ounces

11. M 7 pints
    E 1 gallon

12. R 16 cups
    I 7 pints

13. B 5 fluid ounces
    C 8 tablespoons

—— —— —— ⎯ —— —— ⎯ —— —— —— —— —— ⎯ .
1   2   3   4   5   6   7   8   9   10   11   12   13

Illustration: Michael Austin

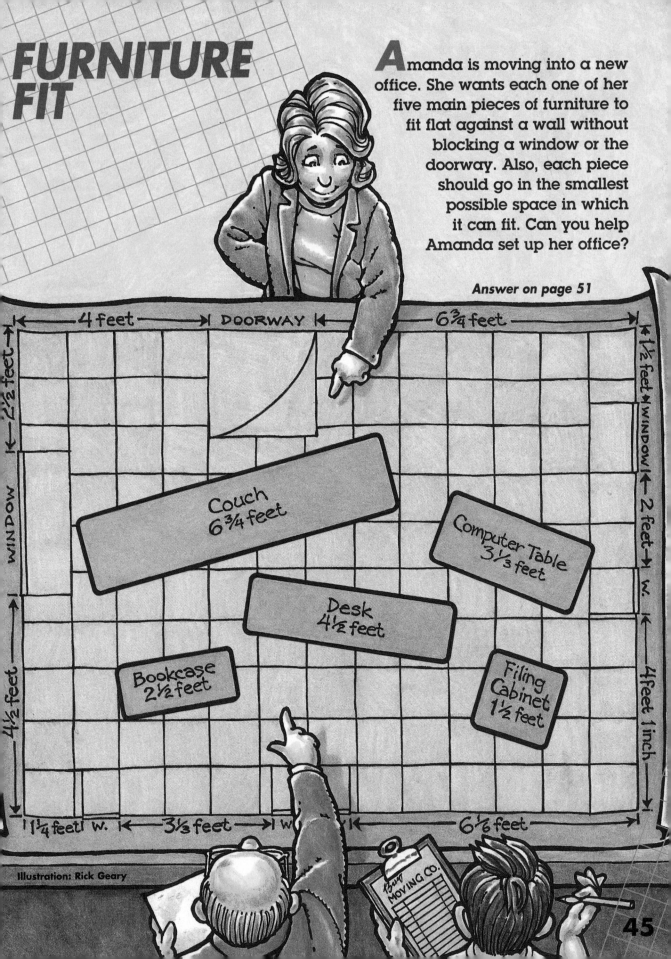

FURNITURE FIT

Amanda is moving into a new office. She wants each one of her five main pieces of furniture to fit flat against a wall without blocking a window or the doorway. Also, each piece should go in the smallest possible space in which it can fit. Can you help Amanda set up her office?

Answer on page 51

4 feet · DOORWAY · 6¾ feet

2½ feet

1½ feet WINDOW 2 feet w.

WINDOW

Couch 6¾ feet

Computer Table 3⅓ feet

Desk 4½ feet

4½ feet

Bookcase 2½ feet

Filing Cabinet 1½ feet

4 feet 1 inch

1¼ feet w. · 3⅓ feet · w. · 6⅙ feet

Illustration: Rick Geary

HINTS AND BRIGHT IDEAS

*T*hese hints may help with some of the trickier puzzles.

COVER
One pound equals 16 ounces.

DIAMOND IN THE ROUGH (page 6)
Number 1 goes in the middle, and 3 goes on the top.

MARBLE MYSTERY (pages 8-9)
Some groups are based on color or design. Others are based on size.

CIRCLE 17 (page 10)
One section has only the number 17 in it.

FUNCTION MACHINES (page 14)
What needs to happen to the first number to turn it into the second number? For instance, on machine C, the second number is $\frac{2}{3}$ of the first number.

FAMOUS NAME (page 15)
Some of the books I wrote include *Kidnapped* and *The Strange Case of Dr. Jekyll and Mr. Hyde.*

WATCH THE DIFFERENCE (pages 16-17)
Remember that all times are between noon and midnight of the same day.

STACKING STANLEY (pages 18-19)
One of Arnold's flavors is Orange Slurp.

THINKING CAP (page 20)
Start small. Try 11 × 11. Next try 111 × 111. See a pattern?

DIGIT DOES IT (pages 22-23)
The word *Inspector* appears in the note's greeting. Use the code numbers from this word to help figure out the rest of the message.

CUTUPS (page 24)
One square will remain untouched. The other squares will get one cut each.

ALL IN A DAY (page 25)
Six hours equal $\frac{1}{4}$ of the day.

LIBRARY LAUGHS (page 28)
Remember to consult the books to find the letter that matches each number.

PHONE FUN (page 29)
Watch your rates for different times of the day.

MATHMAGIC (page 32)
The digits in the ones place do the trick.

MAP MILES (pages 34-35)
Trip 1 includes Blufftown, Cedar Springs, and Lakeside.

ON THE SQUARE (pages 38-39)
Look for smaller rectangular land parcels within each farm. Remember that a square is also a rectangle.

RAINBOW REPORT (page 40)
It may help to write the numbers directly onto each block of color on Alice's report card. To find the average, add together the grades from all the classes. Then divide that total by the number of classes (7).

MASS MATH (page 41)
Pluto has the smallest amount of mass. Jupiter has the greatest amount.

SHAPE MAZE (pages 42-43)
When you move to each new shape, follow the directions on that shape as listed in the key. You need only to add or subtract from the number on the shape you are leaving.

ANSWERS

COVER

4 pounds + 80 ounces (80 ÷ 16 = 5 pounds) + 16 ounces (1 pound) = 10 pounds

PATTERN PIECES (page 3)

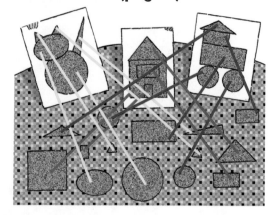

OVER IN THE MEADOW (pages 4-5)

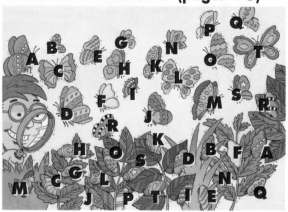

DIAMOND IN THE ROUGH (page 6)

TREE STUMPER (page 7)

A. 18 rings
B. 16 rings
C. 17 rings
D. 15 rings
E. 13 rings

Stump A came from the oldest tree.

MARBLE MYSTERY (pages 8-9)

1. Stripes
2. Small
3. Glassy or clear
4. Chipped
5. Spotted or flecked
6. Solid colors
7. Big
8. Different swirly colors

CIRCLE 17 (page 10)

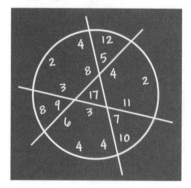

DOTS A LOT (page 11)

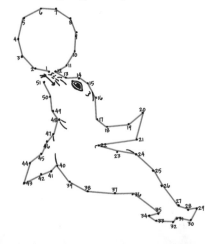

DOGGIE DELIVERY (pages 12-13)

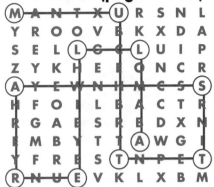

What do dogs like on their pizza?
MUTTS-ARELLA

FUNCTION MACHINES (page 14)

A. Add 2
B. Divide by 6
C. Subtract $\frac{1}{3}$
D. Multiply by 2, then add 1

A		B		C		D	
13	15	36	6	18	12	2	5
7	9	24	4	30	20	3	7
12	14	42	7	6	4	4	9
21	23	12	2	12	8	5	11
26	28	30	5	15	10	6	13

FAMOUS NAME (page 15)

A B C D E F G H I J K L M N O P Q R S T U V

ROBERT LOUIS
STEVENSON

WATCH THE DIFFERENCE (pages 16-17)

5:15—5:55	40 minutes	L
4:55—5:45	50 minutes	O
9:00—10:00	60 minutes	O
7:35—9:00	1 hour, 25 minutes	K
12:30—2:00	1 hour, 30 minutes	M
6:00—8:30	2 hours, 30 minutes	A
2:45—5:30	2 hours, 45 minutes	N
3:00—6:00	3 hours	O
2:40—5:50	3 hours, 10 minutes	H
8:00—11:30	3 hours, 30 minutes	A
7:00—10:45	3 hours, 45 minutes	N
3:45—9:00	5 hours, 15 minutes	D
1:00—10:00	9 hours	S

What did the digital clock
say to its mother?
LOOK, MA! NO HANDS!

STACKING STANLEY (pages 18-19)

1. Pop's gets Strawberry Fizz and
   Berry Bubble (27 + 23 = 50).
2. Arnold's gets Orange Slurp and
   Lefty Lemon (35 + 40 = 75).
3. Mel's gets Go-go Grape and
   Cheery Cherry (22 + 30 = 52).
4. Louie's gets Rah-rah Root Beer and
   Luscious Lime (29 + 31 = 60).

THINKING CAP (page 20)

A. 12,345,678,987,654,321
B. The number of letters in each number word

ODD ORDER (page 21)

AUTOMOBILE starts with gas.

DIGIT DOES IT (pages 22-23)

Dear Inspector Digit,
I flew the coop, so the yolk's on you. I
managed to hide 29 eggs after I hatched
this plan. You'll have to scramble to find
them all.
Al Bumen

a-14	f-19	l-2	r-16	w-22
b-21	g-9	m-4	s-18	y-13
c-7	h-12	n-6	t-20	
d-1	i-15	o-8	u-5	
e-3	k-17	p-10	v-11	

CUTUPS (page 24)

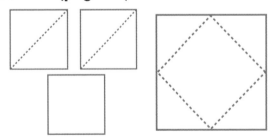

ALL IN A DAY (page 25)

1. Sleep
2. 25%. A day is 24 hours, so 6 hours
   is $\frac{1}{4}$ of that. $\frac{1}{4}$ is equal to 25%.
3. 7—6 hours at school plus 1 hour for
   homework
4. 6 a.m.
5. Jessica spends more time playing
   (3 hours) than volunteering (2 hours).
6. Homework, piano practice, and meals
   equal her playtime (3 hours).

SCRAMBLED PICTURE (pages 26-27)

The Brandenburg Gate in Berlin, Germany

LIBRARY LAUGHS (page 28)

$18 \div 3 = 6$	F	$8 - 6 = 2$	B
$18 - 17 = 1$	A	$5 \times 5 = 25$	Y
$18 + 4 = 22$	V	$3 - 2 = 1$	A
$18 - 3 = 15$	O	$3 \times 6 = 18$	R
$18 \times 1 = 18$	R	$3 + 17 = 20$	T
$18 \div 2 = 9$	I	$3 - 1 = 2$	B
$18 + 2 = 20$	T	$3 \times 7 = 21$	U
$18 - 13 = 5$	E	$3 + 3 = 6$	F
$4 \times 4 = 16$	P	$3 \times 2 = 6$	F
$4 - 3 = 1$	A		
$4 + 5 = 9$	I	FAVORITE PAINTINGS	
$4 + 10 = 14$	N	by Art Buff	
$10 \times 2 = 20$	T		
$10 - 1 = 9$	I		
$10 + 4 = 14$	N		
$10 - 3 = 7$	G		
$10 + 9 = 19$	S		

PHONE FUN (page 29)

Monday, 2/1	$\$.25 \times 35 = \$8.75$
Wednesday, 2/3	$\$.10 \times 56 = \$5.60$
Friday, 2/5	$\$.25 \times 5 = \$1.25$
Saturday, 2/6	$\$.05 \times 65 = \$3.25$
Tuesday, 2/9	$\$.10 \times 42 = \$4.20$
Friday, 2/12	$\$.10 \times 90 = \$9.00$
Sunday, 2/14	$\$.05 \times 5 = \$.25$
Monday, 2/15	$\$.25 \times 10 = \$2.50$
Thursday, 2/18	$\$.25 \times 20 = \$5.00$
Sunday, 2/21	$\$.05 \times 35 = \$1.75$
Tuesday, 2/23	$\$.10 \times 45 = \$4.50$
Friday, 2/26	$\$.25 \times 23 = \$5.75$

February's bill comes to $51.80.
Phyllis went over her budget.

IT FIGURES (pages 30-31)

A—G	D—E	I—L
B—N	H—K	J—M
C—F		

MATHMAGIC (page 32)

The trick is to look only at the last digit of each number chosen. When an odd number is multiplied by an even number, the answer will always be even. When an odd number is multiplied by an odd number, the answer will always be odd. When an even number is multiplied by an even number, the answer will always be even.

To really amaze your friends, let them use calculators to do their figuring. You should still be faster at knowing whether the answer is odd or even.

SAND ART (page 33)

MAP MILES (pages 34-35)

Trip 1—45 miles (Eagle Tower to Blufftown to Cedar Springs to Lakeside to Rapid River to Sandtown)

Trip 2—19 miles (Wood to Pine City to Lakeside)

Trip 3—31 miles (Blue City to Big Bay to Rapid River to Lakeside to Cedar Springs)

Trip 4—27 miles (Big Bay to Pine City to Rockville to Blufftown)

Trip 5—20 miles (Rapid River to Lakeside to Rockville)

FUNNY FRACTIONS (page 36)

DISGUISE: AIRPLANES AND BIRDS BELONG IN THIS

COLOR BY NUMBERS (page 37)